Taking the Fear Out of Learning How to Swim

Martin "Marty" Urand

Taking the Fear Out of Learning

How to Swim

Copyright 2023 by Martin "Marty" Urand

Copyright © Case # 1-12465200681.

Taking the Fear Out of Learning How to Swim

All rights reserved. No part of this publication may be produced, distributed, or transmitted in any form or by any means, including photocopying, recording, or other electronic or mechanical methods, without the prior written permission of the published, except in the case of brief quotations embodied in critical reviews and other noncommercial uses permitted by copyright law.

Paperback ISBN: 978-1-961392-48-9
Hardcover ISBN: 978-1-961392-42-7

The views expressed in this book are solely those of the author and do not necessarily reflect the views of the publisher, and the publisher hereby disclaims any responsibility for them.

USA

Urand Sports Association, Inc.

Urand@ymail.com

About the Author

Unfortunately for me, I learned how to swim under the Brooklyn Bridge! I was self-taught along with other friends of mine who were looking for some thrills during a typical New York hot summer day.

As I remember back to those days, it was despite "fear" that we each learned how to swim. There were two very large boulders at the foot of the bridge. The game that we made up was fairly simple as rules go. Make it from one boulder to the other before a very large water rat takes a bite out of us!

The water depth was not that deep, but we didn't want too much of our bodies submerged in the water for the rodents to have opportunities to snack on. So, on the count of three, we would jump in and we would all flail from one large rock to the other. Despite the danger and thrills that it provided, later in life we all agreed it wasn't a smart way to learn a life-long skill!

Martin "Marty" Urand

In my teenage years, I gradually learned better swimming techniques, and I became a lifeguard on Rockaway Beach, Queens, New York. I worked as a lifeguard until I went off to college in Texas on a basketball scholarship- and subsequently would win a National Championship. I accepted employment again as a lifeguard in the heart of that small, college town of Edinburg, Texas at the popular, local hotel.

Although the pool was not utilized nearly enough to keep me in the stand, I was able to offer my teaching services to a family or two each day. I am sure it was my positive attitude and cordial personality that gravitated families (and sometimes adults) to me. Within minutes, I would parlay my knowledge of swimming into swimming instruction for their young children to learn how to swim, usually in one afternoon of instruction.

I made agreements with potential customers that they would pay me twenty-five dollars if their child could swim the width of the pool within one hour. It never took that long, not even half that time to reach our goal. My secret weapon never failed; I would make up games and activities to keep their children's minds from any water fears that the children might have.

Fifty-eight years later, I am still teaching swimming lessons and still loving every minute of it! Even though I have learned so many teaching techniques, I still feel that my initial, unique teaching skills, and a warm, understanding personality can go a long way toward teaching children and adults how to swim properly. Above all, I learned to respect everyone's fears concerning their safety!

Over my extensive years of teaching swimming, I have coached many swim teams and developed numerous championship teams and individuals. But paramount to my successes as a swim coach, it is the "number of lives" that I have saved during all these years that really floats my boat!

Table of Contents

About the Author	3
ACKNOWLEDGEMENTS	6
Swim Lessons	7
INTRODUCTION	10
PREREQUISITE FOR LEARNING HOW TO SWIM	12
STEP ONE	15
STEP TWO	17
STEP THREE	22
STEP FOUR	24
STEP FIVE	27
STEP SIX	29
STEP SEVEN	31
STEP EIGHT	35
STEP NINE	39
STEP TEN	40

Martin "Marty" Urand

ACKNOWLEDGEMENTS

Much love and thanks to my lovely wife Pamela for her continual support and time editing this publication.

My sincere thanks for the art illustrations from "Rubi" Alvarez

(Caney Creek HS, Conroe ISD, Texas)

SWIM LESSONS

Coach Marty Urand

Welcome to My Swim Classes at April Sound!

Teaching swimming was not my main sport; basketball was my forte. I grew up in New York, Brooklyn (Coney Island). In my senior year of high school, I received a basketball scholarship to UTPA in Edinburg, Texas. I moved from the "Big Apple" to a small college town in The Lower Rio Grande Valley of South Texas, that sits just 20 minutes from the U.S.- Mexico border. After graduating from college, I continued to stay in Texas.

My early life in high school and college were overwhelmed with basketball and schooling. During the summer of my freshman year at UTPA, I took a lifeguarding position at the Echo Hotel, in Edinburg, Texas. Yes, it was a lifeguarding position, but there were very few swimmers at the hotel pool. When a young patron of the hotel sauntered to the pool, I would soon find myself in conversations with their parents, offering suggestions on how to get their child buoyant. Time after time, the parents pulled out a $10 or a $20 bill and insisted I teach their child to swim.

Soon thereafter, when seeing a new potential customer, I would jump in the pool and teach the youngster (or sometimes adult) how to swim. After approaching the parents, I would convince the parents to allow me an hour to teach their child how to swim. If I couldn't get their child to learn how to swim within that hour; they owed me nothing. Almost all the time, I had their child swimming across the width of the pool in half the time. My adult clients and parents realized that my swim techniques were innovative, and my techniques didn't appear in the "how to books" that they read.

Helping people of all ages to learn how to swim while I lifeguarded at the Echo Hotel, in the small border town of Edinberg, Texas, made me feel appreciated; and the extra work was very lucrative.

This added recognition encouraged and spring boarded me to becoming a swim coach for swim teams. I continued teaching swimming; and in a short time, I began to take on coaching swim teams during the summers.

Meanwhile, I coached high school and later college basketball teams in Edinburg. And before too long, my household increased to include two daughters. All family members began assisting me at our family pool at our house, and I would spend many summers teaching swimming at our home.

One of my two daughters has two children. Years ago, when my grandchildren were younger, I began working with my grandson when he was a toddler. I immediately taught him how to swim, which became super-publicity in their neighborhood; and neighbors started seeking swimming lessons for their children at my daughter's home, which lasted fifteen years! Then when my granddaughter became a toddler, not only was I teaching her how to swim, but I was also teaching everyone in the neighborhood how to swim!

Moving the clock forward, I'm a young-at-heart 80-year-old; and, I am currently teaching swimming at our neighborhood pool, April Sound Country Club in Conroe, Texas! It's here, at my current location, where I started daydreaming and brainstorming on writing this publication to share with others my unique swimming techniques.

My swimming techniques work for everyone from 5 years to 85 plus years! The greater my customers' fears, the greater the challenges are for me! It seems like I taught every member of my immediate and extended family how to swim, and fast-forwarding, thousands have passed through my tutelage. I take great pride in teaching children and adults these life-saving life-skills!

INTRODUCTION

Respecting the Learner's Fears

What I have learned from 50 plus years of teaching swimming is:

When teaching others to swim, respect the learners' fears!

It has always been easy for me to teach my students how to swim. So, it is my primary intention, and the goal of this publication, to teach *you* how to teach others how to swim, whether your learner is children or adults. When the learner is ready, any technique can work. If the learner has reservations, or an unwillingness to get into the water-because of fear, that person is a challenge to teach!

I know what I am talking about because for the last *fifty*-eight years I have taught swimming at almost every level. For example, I have coached five-year-old champions, innumerous five-year-old petrified learners, and several 85-year-olds, who just wanted to learn how to swim.

It seems that many of the children who need swimming instructions have one similar characteristic: Fear! So, when giving swim lessons I taught myself how to slow down, and most of all, "Respect their Fear." In this book, you will learn how to teach your learner how to swim using these unique methods I developed for building aquatic skills and promoting confidence in the learner when in the water, so that moving forward is both fun and productive.

The "fear factor" is probably 100% the cause for children being reluctant to learn how to swim. So, asking a child to get comfortable or relax in the water is a tall task to achieve! However, safety, of course, is the main reason everyone wants to learn how to swim. Parenthetically, according to research, approximately 236,000 deaths (globally) are attributed to drownings every year.

Because of these facts, it is essential to teach students who are learning how to swim methods to conquer their fear! Providing aquatic knowledge and instruction along with provisions on how to conquer the fear of the water is *essential* in the process of learning how to swim. Since each person's personality is different, teaching each learner how to swim is different. In regards to handling their fear level, it is so important to respect students' fear levels and place your lesson plans on "hold" until the learner has reached a comfort level.

It is instrumental to begin evaluating the amount of fear the child or adult possess as they enter the water. The fear, of course, is the thought of drowning. Water, in general, will float everything that has air in it! But trying to teach this is basically impossible, at this point in the learning cycle. Nevertheless, it really will not take long to teach this, if your student is comfortable with you, and trusts you aren't going to move faster than they are prepared to do.

The location of swimming lessons is vitally important. The chances of learning how to swim in the ocean or a murky lake will inhibit learning. A crystal-clear pool with a shallow end will increase the chances of learning and becoming comfortable with the learner. When entering the water with the learner, a first and foremost prerequisite for the first goal of instruction to be attainable, create the scaffolding for the learner to have a positive attitude and feel happy.

PREREQUISITE FOR LEARNING HOW TO SWIM

How to Teach "Having Fun/Happiness While Learning to Swim"

The following are some suggestions for creating a "fun/happy environment":

- Begin with talking with the learner on the steps of the shallow end of the pool to begin developing their confidence by assuring them that we will NOT be going underwater today.

Spend as much time as needed to create a strong bond. Trust is the "Key" to developing their confidence and Self-esteem.

1. Tell your student, "Hold my hands and let's explore the pool." Pull the student through the water while talking about the pool, or directing their attention to others in the pool or locations that you plan to use for your teaching.

2. "Let's see how strong you are by climbing out of the pool." Teach them to place both hands on the side of the pool and bring their knee up onto the deck, then the other knee and stand up. Explain the importance of knowing how to get out of the pool. In a few lessons, you will be teaching another method for climbing out of the pool that will increase their strength and flexibility.

3. Constantly talk to your students keeping their mind engaged on the sights and sounds of the pool, rather than entertaining their fears, etc. **"Praise what you want to raise!"**

4. Gently scoop up water and place it on their arms, while constantly asking the child if they are doing ok. They MUST feel that you are 100% concerned about them and their feelings.

5. Ask your student the following questions:

> "Let's try and make friends with the water."
>
> "What do you want to say to the water?"
>
> "Is the water 'uncomfortable' to you?"

"Did you know that water helps you in so many ways?"

I usually tell my students about the story of a sunken submarine that was in the ocean. A company was wanting to raise the sub up using very big and heavy equipment, bringing the sub to the top surface, but nothing worked. Then they filled the sub with air, and the sub floated to the top of the ocean.

"Did you know that air can bring anything under water up no matter how heavy or light it may be?"

"Do you have air in you?"

"Sure, you do! That is why if you have your mouth and nose closed, you cannot sink! It is like magic!"

Push a ball the size of a volleyball down under water with your hand and release it watching the ball shoot up from under the water.

I realize that getting your learner to relax and start having fun with the swim lesson is certainly easier said than done! Nevertheless, take **ALL** the time necessary to create a warm, positive atmosphere where "happiness" can be reached.

I have shared several skills that are perceived as "fun". When I am teaching academic teachers in the classroom, I use this quote on many occasions. ***"WE DON'T TEACH FUN, BUT FUN IS THE PRODUCT OF GOOD TEACHING".***

Taking the Fear Out of Learning How to Swim

STEP ONE

Learning the Best Position for Swimming

Verbal Ques:

- **Superman** is the position that I want the learner to become familiar with. Arms stretched upward and legs straight (prone position). In many cases, students have never experienced a prone position. Floats, tubes and even life jackets promote a vertical position (legs downward) and become anxious when their legs are up, giving a feeling of tipping over.

By teaching your student how to lift their legs, kicking will become easier to teach. Superman to the rescue!

So, the **FIRST STEP** is just simply allowing the student to hold your arm, and with your other arm, hold the student in a "slight" prone position.

Allow your learner to become comfortable with you, walking backwards with their legs somewhere between pointing down and feet on top of the water. The learner becomes nervous when they feel they are going to fall forward into the water. It is very advanced for a learner to accomplish a prone position in the initial trials. Be patient with this skill!

Gradually increase the horizontal level of their legs toward the prone position. You can use a floating device placed under their midsection, while you hold their hands and propel them through the water. Repeat this method and reduce the floating devices, until they are comfortable in a prone position without any floating devices holding them up.

When the swimmer is comfortable in a prone position, you can begin teaching the kick/motor (**STEP TWO**).

STEP TWO
The Kick (Motor)

Verbal Ques:

The **SECOND STEP** and most important skill in learning how to swim is the kick. I like to call this "your motor". The motor needs to be practiced at each of your lessons.

Basically, the kick/motor allows the swimmer to keep their legs up by kicking downward. Mention to them about what happened to the ball when it was pushed down. Anything that is pushed downward will cause the body to rise, whether it is their arms or legs.

Learning the proper kick (motor) is very important towards becoming buoyant. The learner will want to kick bending their knees slightly. Use your arms to assist with their legs starting downward and upward kicking from their hips and not their knees.

As you teach the learner how to swim, spend as much time as possible to obtain strong kicking motions from your student.

By bending their knees too much, they will be splashing, kicking, and placing more water on their lower back, and that will make moving in the water difficult. The more they kick down, the more they will stay on top of the water. Let the swimmer hold your shirt with both arms, and that will free your arms to work with their legs to help them feel the proper kick/motor motion.

As their motor becomes stronger, students holding a floating noddle can move on their own through the water.

Have the swimmer hold and use a "noddle" to develop their confidence by not holding you.

Require that the swimmer keeps their arms straight while holding the noddle. The swimmer, by utilizing their motor to keep their body on top of the water, will develop more confidence and strength.

This will increase the total body prone position that will enhance the ability to swim.

The motor is the most important skill to learn at this point in the learning process.

We discussed the first two steps without mentioning "Going under water"! This usually is a major fear for most learners. Respect their fears! Work on their confidence and self-esteem with small tasks; the learner's confidence will add up quickly.

The big question always arises as to how fast to go when teaching swimming. My answer is to get to know your learner. If they are fast moving, jumping around, not letting some splashing bother them, then I would consider these actions to allow for a "Fast track course".

On the other hand, a learner that is pulling their head away from splashing and moving slowly in order not to stir up the water, then a "slower track" is necessary. **"Respect their fears!"**

Each day needs to be "similar" to the previous lesson. I like to begin with reviewing their accomplished skills, do some motor work, then add a new skill to the learning process.

Since starting lessons, the learner has always faced you. It is a good time to hold the learner with your hands under their arms/hips with their back of their head toward your face. Be sure to consistently talk to your learner while in this new position. They are usually not comfortable and need plenty of encouragement, while facing away from you.

You can ask the learner if they would like to hold your hand while in this position. Make note when they let go, this is a positive step toward gaining their independence.

Also, I like for the student to hold the back of my shirt or neck while they kick. This is another way for the learner to build confidence- that they are achieving skills without the teacher watching them. It is a little step, but these little steps can go a long way towards building confidence (which is the name of the game).

As the learner becomes comfortable in these positions, move toward the side of the pool, and ask that they place their feet on your knees and jump toward the wall. The distance is very small, maybe a foot away. I call this the "flying squirrel". Your negotiating skills will come into play as you ask if they can make it to the wall from a small distance away.

> Say to your student, "How about this? Do you think you can jump to the wall of the pool like a 'flying squirrel'?"

Jumping to the wall is a small task but it will go a long way toward building your student's confidence. After successfully jumping to the wall, ask that they push off the wall and come back to you, without going under water. If unwilling, hold their hands and bring them to your shirt from the wall.

I use plenty of praise utilizing this task. My learners absolutely enjoy this and talk about this when they get home.

A neat way to build confidence is teaching the "flying squirrel" technique.

Taking the Fear Out of Learning How to Swim

Jumping to the wall is very exciting for the learner since they are literally moving away from one safety position to gain another safety position. Jumping away from your teacher and having the strength to grab and hold on to the wall is a skill that certainly makes your learner proud of their accomplishments!

Once that maneuver becomes a learned skill, ask your learner to jump back to you, and begin their motor as soon as they begin this step. This procedure usually creates splashing here and there, in which you don't acknowledge. It is VERY IMPORTANT: Don't turn your head when your learner jumps toward you, causing a splash. It's a bit risky that if you turn away, you might miss catching them. No room for error when building a child's confidence!

Negotiating is an important skill to utilize, as you continue encouraging your learner to take more and more little steps, that will add up quickly. I call these little steps "splinter skills". Each step is part of the whole, and it comes together when all the small steps are learned.

Finally, I turn around so that my back is facing the learner, and ask that they jump on my back. (Be sure to be very close to your student!)

I would ask them, "Did you make it?"

I pretend I am looking for them in the water, while asking, "Where are you?"

When my learner tries to be seen, I look the other way, and give the impression that I don't know where they are. I pretend I am concerned, while raising my voice, "Where are you?"

"Are you there?" This playful game is very popular, and results in lots of laughter (which you really want).

After playing this game, stay in that position, and have your student use their "motor" to go across the pool holding the bottom of your shirt.

STEP THREE
Blowing Bubbles

Verbal Ques:

Taking air in and blowing air out are two, very different skills to practice. Taking air in is performed above the water, and releasing the air is performed under water by blowing air out.

Taking in water through your nose or mouth is a sure way to get into trouble and scare anyone!

So, teaching your student how to blow bubbles using a straw is **STEP THREE**. Then, demonstrate this step using your mouth instead of a straw. Be sure to show your learner that making sounds as you blow into the water is fun! As this skill becomes easier, demonstrate to your learner how you are opening your mouth and using your throat muscles to not allow water to go down your throat.

A super method to teach the first phase of exchanging air is to teach how to blow the "old "air out by using a straw.

The rationale of blowing air under water is to make the "air exchange" very easy for your student(s) to learn. By releasing the air before you need it will reduce one step from the air exchange.

The reduction comes from not having to release the old air before taking in new air above water.

By releasing the air under water, air will flow into the swimmer's mouth as soon as their head comes out of the water.

Again, every little accomplishment in these techniques creates an opportunity for *your* students' self-esteem to improve. Over the years, I have seen children's personalities change drastically by accomplishing very small water tasks, and their increased confidence from their newly acquired aquatic abilities are self-evident.

The next area that needs to be addressed is getting your learner's legs to become prone in the water. Usually, most floating devices require the legs to be pointed downward in a walking position. This type of position is almost impossible for learning how to swim. Once a student learns how to swim, I teach survival skills that include "treading water".

Treading water is taught in a walking position or in a prone position. But for the most part, legs need to be behind, kind of a "Superman" in a flying position that we previously addressed.

STEP FOUR
Going Under Water

Verbal Ques:

Here it is, **STEP FOUR,** your learner's first attempt towards going underwater. I start by having the learner wear goggles, not a face mask. The goggles should not cover their nose.

I place the goggles on the learner by placing the eye piece over their eyes then placing the strap over their head, just below the crown of their head. When your learner is wearing their goggles, go through some of the motor drills, as they become familiar with wearing goggles. Note, working on the motor drills also takes their mind off having to go underwater.

Please remember to "respect their fears" because this is the "**big one**"!

Depending on how comfortable the learner is wearing the goggles will determine whether I start the swim lesson with the student learning how to go underwater today or not.

If the student is having difficulty getting used to wearing the goggles, I may have to make changes to my swim lesson plan, and modify this lesson, replacing it with giving a remedial swim lesson. If this is the situation, I practice only the previous swimming skills they've learned.

If the student takes readily to wearing the googles, then the day has come, and we need to start the procedure for going underwater.

I would begin by having the student lie down on the steps of the pool and have the student look at their hands underwater.

Taking the Fear Out of Learning How to Swim

Have your student focus on how the water acts as a magnifying glass when looking at objects under water. Be sure to have your students take their time, and don't be in a rush with this step! You are at a fork in the road and in danger of losing a student if you go too fast.

Because of their nerves, your student's instinct when going under water is to sniff in. That sniff allows the water to be drawn in through their nose and that is very uncomfortable. So, spend plenty of time teaching your students how to close their mouth and nose, while you submerge them where the water comes to the bottom of their goggles. Repeat until you can see that the learner is not pulling back when you lower them in the water.

Tell your student to blow some bubbles through their mouth and then through their nose. (Ask them to blow through their nose a few times out of the water), before asking them to try it in the very shallow water. Keep their mind on looking at how the water changes the appearance of objects, such as a penny or any object under water.

Being able to keep their eyes open underwater borders on a form of magic to a novice swimmer. Always hold their hand, arm, or side as they go under and explore below the surface of the water. You can go under with them and see if their eyes are open in the eye piece of their goggles.

To a child, being able to keep their eyes open and see "clearly" underwater is "magical"; you could have fun with this skill!

Another good drill is to get submerging rings or colorful sticks that float just below the surface, and have the swimmer reach for the objects while their head is under the water. "Practice makes perfect." Once this drill of going under and seeing below the surface, the swimmer will begin having fun!

At this point, learning to go underwater is the "**deal breaker**"!

Go slowly. Know your learner and again, respect their fears.

STEP FIVE
Breath Control

Verbal Ques:

Breath control is the next step (**STEP FIVE**) toward conquering the fear of learning how to swim and swimming. Start with counting to two, and bring your eyes and face out of the water. ALWAYS, tell your learner to blow the water away from their mouth when coming out of the water. This will keep the water from going into their mouth.

Practice at the steps on the side of the pool, while they master this skill. Once you feel they are comfortable, try doing this procedure away from the steps. The goal is to count underwater to five and then ten. You can go underwater with them and look at each other, making faces and laughing when you come up.

For example, you can ask your student, "How about practicing your 'motor' while under water for a five count?"

Once they accomplish kicking while underwater, go back to the wall and practice going underwater and kicking to the wall. Make sure you tell them once they touch the wall, to **"Let their hands do the walking"** up the wall to safety.

This is MAJOR! (Towards swim proofing them).

Emphasize to your student the point of NOT stopping their motor until they have reached safety (the top tile, and not just touch the wall tile). Too many children touch the wall and stop their "motors" and bounce off the wall and have a difficult time restarting their "motors" because their legs (motor) are sinking.

Remember, getting the learner to be in a swimming position (prone position from head to feet) is your goal. The ability to swim is almost impossible when the learner is not in a prone position.

At this point, your student is now moving in the water and getting from one place to another. Avoid asking your student to motor toward the steps. The problem becomes that they will shut their "motors" off as they get to the steps. With this in mind, I teach in water depth that is above the height of the learner and my mid-section.

A super skill to practice is to ask the swimmer to push off the wall and motor to me (with their head in the water) and grab my shirt.

Once they reach your shirt, lift them up to get air and push them back to the wall. Remind them to keep their "motor" on until their hand walks up the wall and reaches safety. Safety is when their hand grabs the top of the wall. At this point, they can stop their motor and rest, while holding the top side of the pool.

Do this several times before taking a break and taking the goggles off. Teach them how to spit inside the lenses to avoid fogging up their goggles.

Now, your learner has the skills for moving in the water using their "motor", holding their breath while being under water. The learner is very proud of their water skills and looking forward to the next aquatic skill to be learned.

STEP SIX
Basic Floating Concepts

Verbal Ques:

- Hold an "X"
- Parachute Jump

STEP SIX is very important towards the entire concept of your learner feeling comfortable in the water. It is the floating concept, but not on their back. I usually save that for last, since it takes the most confidence to perform in the water.

The official name of this face down, prone float is called the "dead man's float". I choose to call it the "parachute jump" or "X".

I ask the learner to **close their mouth and hold their breath** during this exercise (10-15 seconds) with their head facing down, and imagine that they just jumped out of a plane, and they are looking down at the earth (bottom of the pool). The point is made after a few trials that the water is very friendly and will aways keep you up and not let you sink (providing the swimmer holds their air in)!

This is a "must" skill to teach! It allows your student to realize that the water WILL keep you up and not sink!

STEP SEVEN
Using Your Arms

Verbal Ques:

- **Paddle** – The arm/hand that is used to pull the water under and behind the swimmer.
- **Home Plate** – Where both arms start out before taking a stroke.
- **Hit the wall** – An imaginary wall that the arm that is taking the stroke hits and slides up causing the elbow to surface above the water.
- **Grasshopper Leg** – When the elbow surfaces above the water line and resembles a grasshopper's leg.

STEP SEVEN is teaching the use of the learner's arms. An important thought to keep in mind is that the circular arm movements can be divided into two parts.

The first is the pull (forward motion and pushing downward). This is the productive movement.

The second phase is the recovery or returning your arm up to the top of the water (home plate). This is a non-productive movement.

The key with each pull is to allow the elbow to come out of the water after hitting the imaginary wall. When the elbow comes out of the water it resembles a "grasshopper's leg".

Teach the student to pull until their hand touches the imaginary wall, and slide hand upward so that the elbow comes up through the water.

There are two parts of the second movement of the circle motion that can cause problems:

First, bringing your arms up pushes the learner down, due to the upward motion against the water, that results in the body being pushed away from the top of the water, and makes it difficult to bring the second arm up for the second pull.

Secondly, it places too much tension on the shoulder joint. Over time, the tension will take its toll on the swimmer's rotator cuff.

Taking the Fear Out of Learning How to Swim

Using the deck of the pool to maneuver your student for teaching some swimming techniques is very beneficial towards learning the proper arm and leg movements.

This stroke is called the "free style" and should be taught with both arms in the "Superman" flying position. Each arm begins on "home plate" waiting to take its turn to "pull".

Each "pull" has two parts: The "pull" begins with a downward motion with the hand in a flat (to move more water downward) position. This movement continues a downward motion until the arm hits an imaginary wall at the bottom of the "pull".

Next, the palm of the hand will touch the (Imaginary) wall, and the elbow will bend so that that the elbow will come up and out of the water, which will be followed by the hand.

The elbow comes out first, then the hand, in that order. Tell your swimmer that the elbow creates a hole for the hand to come out of.

If the hand comes out of the water from any other place than the "elbow hole", it will not be correct!

Once the hand reaches forward and touches the water (home plate), the other hand/arm will perform the same stroke. I like to tell the learner that their hands are on home plate together and will wait there until the first arm "pulls" and returns to home before the second arm begins its "pull" motion.

The purpose of the arms coming back to home plate is to allow each arm to perform its function, and not allow the arms to go too fast and create an agitating movement, which will create a negative reaction toward moving forward.

Teaching the arms and "motor" together at first will require a lot of concentration, and therefore I do not teach the "air" phase at this point. It becomes too busy to include air at this point. I assist them on the 4th stroke to lift them up to take in air.

It is **very important** to have the learner release the old air underwater on the 3rd stroke. Once the old air is released, obtaining new air will be simple on the 4th stroke.

I like to teach each arm stroke having a number. The right arm is number one, left is number two, right arm is number three (blow air under water), and the fourth stroke is the air stroke.

My cadence count that I go over and over is: Pull, pull, blow, and air!

Have the swimmer repeat that cadence with you several times.

An excellent method of teaching the proper technique is to place the student on the side of the pool with their left arm dangling off the side of the pool and the right arm lying on the deck.

This position allows me to hold the learner's arms and guide their arms through the swimmer's stroke cycle.

Taking the Fear Out of Learning How to Swim

STEP EIGHT
Doggy Paddle (for Getting Air)

That brings us to **STEP EIGHT,** getting air. Teaching your learner how to get air begins with their head in the water. Tap the learner on their head and direct your student to blow the old air out under water. The learner must know that they need to get rid of their "old air" first before "new air" can be taken in and used. In other words, taking in air over and over will not be usable air. **Old air must be released first before new air can be used.**

Teaching your student how to "doggy paddle" is a fail-safe way to show the learner that air can be taken in at any point while they're in the water.

The "doggy paddle" is performed while in a prone position, moving the arms in a small circle in the water just under their chest. The head needs to be out of the water. I ask that the learner barks like a dog or talks to me while performing this skill. Have your learner practice this skill while asking the learner to follow you around the pool.

The speed of their arms can be slow- under control- and not fast!

Now let's put it together:

Call out to your student, "Arms at "home plate."

"Begin the stroke by counting one, two, three, air, and fourth stroke. "

"Let's try to get eight strokes- which will require two times to get air."

"Now we will try twelve strokes and three airs!"

This is a perfect time to practice "blow and go". The purpose of this drill is to have the learner exchange air. Holding the learner's hands, the learner will practice blowing bubbles, and then lifting their head out of the water (performing the doggy paddle) and taking in new air.

Practice this drill many times, as the swimmer will become more and more comfortable with the rhythmic movements of exchanging old air for new air.

Next, let the swimmer perform the drill without holding their hands. Completing their four-stroke cycle, which includes blowing bubbles (old air) and on the third stroke and doggy paddle for new air. After several practices, the swimmer is now ready for the next step.

Learning how to breathe in a rhythmic motion takes practice. When the "fourth" arm (air arm) begins to pull, and the elbow comes out of the water, is when the new air is taken.

This can be practiced by holding your learner's hands, while in a prone position. Gently squeeze hand one, then squeeze number two, "three", and they turn their head to the left. Be sure to keep watching to see if bubbles are released under water on the third squeeze.

The side of the learner's head should rest in the water (right ear in the water), while getting new air from their mouth. Practice this many times before taking a rest. Then practice again, while the learner is in a "controlled" position. This rhythm is difficult while swimming, so practice in this controlled position as much as possible, so that this skill can be achieved while in this unique position.

After practicing breathing for a few lessons, it is time to practice the learner swimming to you. I like to measure the distance that I want them to swim in, taking a number of airs. So, let's begin with the swimmer exchanging air two times. That is eight strokes, with each fourth stroke resulting in taking air.

Practice the two-air distance, four or five times before moving to three or more airs. Once your learner swims to you, and you verbally reward their effort, I like to place the student on their back, while supporting them totally. I ask them to go to "sleep" (pretend) and keep their belly up to the surface of the water. I keep the side of my head next to theirs and talk to them the entire time.

Floating on the back takes the most confidence and the swimmer will want to bring their head up, which causes their midsection to sink. Place your hand under their head as you talk to them, reminding them to keep their head back. I even try and use my other hand to shade their eyes, so they are more comfortable.

After many practices on their back, I tell the student to try and float for three seconds. Reassuring them that in the floating position, with air present in their body, they will be like a balloon and unable to sink.

Careful! If student's head and chin drop too far back, water could enter their nose and produce an uncomfortable feeling, that could prevent further learning the float.

Knowing these signs of discomfort and assisting the learner to avoid negative feelings about the water will assure the learner that you aware of their feelings. The more confidence they have in you, the more confidence they will gain themselves.

STEP NINE
Developing Strength and Endurance

STEP NINE is developing strength and endurance. There are several ways to accomplish this, depending on many factors. The pool size pool can affect the training. In a small home pool that is rectangular or circular, the swimmer can begin with swimming laps from side to side. Adding a lap each time they complete the goal is something that you and the swimmer can negotiate.

I like to finish my class with lap work, keeping a record of the learner's number of mastered laps from day to day.

If the pool is larger and performing a lap is too difficult, have the learner swim half of the pool, or allow the learner to stand, or hold on to them, giving them a rest break before starting the next portion. This is perfect when working in a community pool, and there is a lane for swimmers. It may take eight rest stops before completing. Each day you would want to count the number of fewer rests, until the swimmer can swim the entire 25 feet/yards.

STEP TEN
Survival Skills (Water Proofing)

STEP TEN is about teaching survival skills. I use this term rather than referring to it as "water proofing".

Depending on the age of the swimmer, different techniques can be taught. For students that are five and older, the most respected method for staying afloat is called "scaling" or "treading water".

This movement is performed in a standing position. This means that the swimmer's position is in a standing position which at the beginning of lessons, we are trying to avoid. (At that point, we were trying to break the habit of standing as we practiced the importance of being in the prone position.)

So, if the swimmer is still a novice and having a difficult time keeping their legs up, I would encourage not teaching treading water at this time.

A safer way to begin this survival skill is to perform an enhanced doggy paddle position in a prone position, and gradually lower the legs toward the vertical (standing position) position.

If the swimmer is ready, begin with the legs, while holding either your hand or the side of the pool. This movement resembles riding a bicycle. Both legs are moving in circular movements. The movement needs to be wider than if riding a bike. The legs while circling, should be outside of the shoulders.

The feeling achieved should feel like pushing against the water, that simultaneously lifts the body in an upward manner. The movement requires the knees to be bent, with the toes flexed (not pointed).

The position of the arms mimics the legs, in that they also are like riding a bicycle. The hands need to be opened, while pushing in a downward motion. In order to maintain a controlled breathing motion for surviving, it requires a lot of energy. The swimmer may want to lightly use their feet and arms, with their head in the water; and when air is needed, increase the energy, and come to the surface for new air.

Using this system will increase the strength and endurance of the learner, granted they are improving to the point of staying above water. As the movements become stronger, the circular movements given from the arms and legs could become very slow, as efficiency is reached.

This skill is best worked on at the end of the lesson because their strength and endurance will be tested before they leave the pool. Practicing at the beginning of the lesson will tire the swimmer and prevent them from not having the energy for learning other swimming skills.

For students that are younger than five years of age, I would teach floating on the stomach (parachute jumps), and moving their hands, as we have taught in the doggy paddle lesson, to bring their head up for new air. You can begin with asking the swimmer to perform for three airs, and gradually move away from counting the airs to work on counting for time. Can the student float for thirty seconds, and then sixty seconds?

I entrust you have enjoyed this instruction book on teaching your learner how to swim. I hope you can use the techniques in this book to increase both your knowledge on how to teach someone to swim, and build-up more confidence to get started on your endeavors of teaching your student to learn how to swim.

We have now completed my publication on the techniques I use to teach my students how to swim. It is now your turn to take this methodology and begin practicing how to teach your learner how to swim. I wish you the best in teaching your newly learned skill: teaching someone how to swim.

Consider yourself a "life saver!"

Autumn and Kolton (Brother & Sister) First Lesson

Taking the Fear Out of Learning How to Swim

Clockwise from top: Vinny, Luke, Noah, Autumn, Kolton, and Coach Marty

"We don't teach fun, but fun is the product of good teaching."

Marty Urand

www.ingramcontent.com/pod-product-compliance
Lightning Source LLC
Chambersburg PA
CBHW041235060526
44107CB00136BA/809